Farm Machines

Cultivators

Connor Dayton

PowerKiDS press

New York

Published in 2012 by The Rosen Publishing Group, Inc.
29 East 21st Street, New York, NY 10010

First Edition

Editor: Jennifer Way
Book Design: Greg Tucker

Photo Credits: Cover, pp. 7, 10–11, 15, 17, 18–19, 24 (top left, bottom) Shutterstock.com; pp. 5, 13, 23, 24 (top right) iStockphoto/Thinkstock; pp. 9, 21 Hemera/Thinkstock.

Library of Congress Cataloging-in-Publication Data

Dayton, Connor.
 Cultivators / by Connor Dayton. — 1st ed.
    p. cm. — (Farm machines)
 Includes index.
 ISBN 978-1-4488-4950-5 (library binding) — ISBN 978-1-4488-5050-1 (pbk.) —
 ISBN 978-1-4488-5051-8 (6-pack)
 1. Cultivators—Juvenile literature. I. Title.
 S683.D39 2012
 631.5'1—dc22

                                    2010050139

Manufactured in the United States of America

CPSIA Compliance Information: Batch #WS11PK: For Further Information contact Rosen Publishing, New York, New York at 1-800-237-9932

Contents

Mix the Dirt   4

Pulling Weeds   12

Big Cultivators   16

Words to Know   24

Index   24

Web Sites   24

Cultivators are farm machines.

Cultivators mix up dirt.
They do this before
crops are planted.

Cultivators mix air into the **soil**. This makes soil loose.

The part that
digs into the
soil is called
the shank.

Cultivators pull weeds, too. They pull the weeds growing between rows.

Tractors pull cultivators.

Some big cultivators fold up. This makes them easier to move.

Big cultivators can work on many rows at once.

Working the soil is
called tilling.

Taking care of the soil is hard work. Cultivators make it easier!

Words to Know

crops

soil

tractor

Index

R

rows, 12, 18

S

soil, 8, 10,
   20, 22

T

tractors, 14

W

weeds, 12

work, 22

Web Sites

Due to the changing nature of Internet links, PowerKids Press has developed an online list of Web sites related to the subject of this book. This site is updated regularly. Please use this link to access the list:
www.powerkidslinks.com/farm/cultiv/